Published by
North Atlantic Books
Huichin, unceded Ohlone land
aka Berkeley, California

Cover art by Rina Deshpande
Cover design by Jasmine Hromjak
Book design by Happenstance Type-O-Rama

Printed in Canada

Yoga Nidra Lullaby is sponsored and published by North Atlantic Books, an educational nonprofit based in the unceded Ohlone land Huichin (*aka* Berkeley, CA) that collaborates with partners to develop cross-cultural perspectives, nurture holistic views of art, science, the humanities, and healing, and seed personal and global transformation by publishing work on the relationship of body, spirit, and nature.

North Atlantic Books' publications are distributed to the US trade and internationally by Penguin Random House Publisher Services. For further information, visit our website at www.northatlanticbooks.com.

Library of Congress Cataloging-in-Publication Data

Names: Deshpande, Rina, author, illustrator.
Title: Yoga Nidra lullaby / words and pictures by Rina Deshpande.
Description: Huichin, unceded Ohlone land aka Berkeley, California : North
    Atlantic Books, [2022] | Audience: Ages 4-8 | Audience: Grades K-1 |
    Summary: "Mindful relaxation cues that help kids use Yoga Nidra
    techniques to fall asleep"— Provided by publisher.
Identifiers: LCCN 2022011436 | ISBN 9781623176976 (hardcover) | ISBN
    9781623176983 (ebook)
Subjects: LCSH: Relaxation—Juvenile literature. | Meditation—Juvenile
    literature. | Yoga—Juvenile literature. | Mind and body—Juvenile
    literature.
Classification: LCC RA785 .D395 2022 | DDC 613.7/046—dc23/eng/20220401
LC record available at https://lccn.loc.gov/2022011436

1 2 3 4 5 6 7 8 9 Friesens 27 26 25 24 23 22

North Atlantic Books is committed to the protection of our environment. We print on recycled paper whenever possible and partner with printers who strive to use environmentally responsible practices.

Yoga Nidra Lullaby

Words and Pictures by **Rina Deshpande**

For my mother

North Atlantic Books
Huichin, unceded Ohlone land
aka Berkeley, California

The orange sun begins to sink.
Skies are golden. Clouds are pink.

What evening colors do you see?

Birds are gliding on a breeze.

Breathe in deeply. Feel at ease.

Can you practice three cycles of deep breathing?   3...2...1.

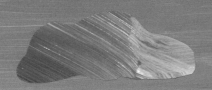

Buzzing cars are winding down.
The night is full of gentle sounds.

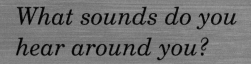

*What sounds do you
hear around you?*

Feel your heartbeat, smooth and calm.
"Goodnight," it thumps under your palm.

What sounds do you hear inside your own body?

Clouds are soft beneath your head.

Snuggle in your fluffy bed.

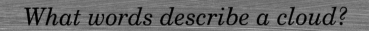

What words describe a cloud?

Heavy eyelids start to fall. The moon looks like a floating ball.

What else does the moon remind you of?

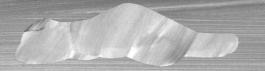

Mist is cool upon your nose.
Sleepy ears begin to doze.

What would you whisper to
someone you love?

Stars reach far across the sky.
Rest your lips. Let out a sigh.

What else can you imagine in the night sky?

Leaves are whirling through the air.
Breezes brush across your hair.

How does wind feel on your skin?

Trees cast shadows in a line.

Roll your shoulders.
Stretch your spine.

*Can you reach your
whole body long?*

Birds are huddled
in their nest.

Calm your belly, back, and chest.

How does it feel to cuddle someone?

Waves expand across the sand. Spread your arms. Relax your hands.

Can you imagine soothing waves?

Skies are clear. Moonlight glows.

Blankets warm your legs and toes.

Can you relax your whole body from head to toe?

Safe and cozy in your room,
let your goodnight wishes bloom.

What is your goodnight wish?

Peace with you and peace with me.
Peace with all the things that be.

Om Shanti. Shanti. Shanti.

Goodnight.

A Note from the Author

Yoga nidra is a comforting way to relax your mind and body, step by step. In the Sanskrit language, *yoga* means "unity," and *nidra* means "sleep." The practice is thousands of years old and comes from India, where my family is from. My roots are Indian, and I am American. I feel happy that people all around the world enjoy yoga nidra.

When I was a child, my mother created a lullaby called "Eyes Go to Sleep." In her gentle song, she wished goodnight to each part of my body from head to toe. This book is my own yoga nidra poem so you can say goodnight to the clouds, the moon, and the leaves outside, and to your eyes, your arms, and your legs as you cuddle up inside.

If your abilities vary from what's offered in this book, please visit *rinathepoet.com* for educational activities and for inclusive modifications, including audio read by me, Rina Deshpande.